Of Tortoises
and Other Jews

Hannah Yakin

Copyright © 2014 Hannah Yakin, Jerusalem, Israel.
All rights reserved

Dutch Title: *Over schildpadden en andere Joden*
Story and illustrations: Hannah Yakin
Photos: from the album of Hannah Yakin
Design: Petra van der Zande

ISBN 978-965-7542-22-4

This book can be ordered by contacting:
⇒ edenj@zahav.net.il
⇒ tsurtsinapublications@gmail.com
⇒ www.Lulu.com
⇒ www.art-yakin.com

Summary:
Hannah Yakin tells about her youth in the Netherlands during the Second World War. Thanks to her non-Jewish father's courage and ingenuity, Jewish Hannah, her mother and two sisters are spared a certain death in the Nazi concentration camps. They even hide many Jews in their home.

Tags:
Second World War; WWII, Jewish persecution, anti-Semitism, Netherlands, Amstelveen, people in hiding, Hunger Winter, Nazis, Amsterdam

Many thanks to my dear friend Petra, for her wonderful help!

A *Tsur Tsina* Production

Printed by PRINTIV, Jerusalem, Israel

In Memory of my Father, Jan van Hulst

(1903-1975)

Seeing three pairs of bare feet sticking out from under the curtains, Mama cried out, "War! War! Stay away from the window!"

May 10, 1940

The noise woke us up. Although the curtains were drawn, we saw streaks of yellow and orange light sweep along our bedroom window as if a giant party was being celebrated in heaven. I don't know what my sisters were imagining, but in my ears resounded our national anthem, played by some celestial fanfare orchestra. The only other time I had seen such a massive display of fireworks was on Queen Wilhelmina's birthday.

Myriam tiptoed towards the window, stooped and disappeared behind the curtains. Her cry of astonishment tuned in with my orchestra. "Look what they are doing!"
A moment later the three of us pressed our noses flat against the window pane. Screeching with excitement, we watched airplanes dive through the dawning sky and aim at each other, shooting balls, red-hot and burning, trailing tails of smoke and fire, exploding into kaleidoscopic configurations.

Like the black slaves in Myriam's history book, who recklessly dived for coins thrown into a whirlpool by their white masters, the airplanes seemed to plunge towards our very window. To watch them chase each other, to see them tumble down in flames over the roofs of Amstelveen, was by far the most exciting thing I had ever seen.

Mama burst into our bedroom and, seeing three pairs of bare feet sticking out from under the curtains, cried out,

"War! War! Stay away from the window!"

Of course we had heard about Hitler, and Papa had been called into the army weeks ago, but life without him was in a way even snugger than before. Every evening Mama put my hair in curl papers so that I would look more like my sisters, and while she did this I had to read aloud in French because Mama came from Belgium and French was her mother tongue. Papa had a gift for foreign languages. So we talked French at home.

Every morning Mama dressed us in identical dresses, as if we were oversized dolls who, in turn, played house with our own dolls under her supervision. Like Mama, we spoke French with our dolls. Like her we had three daughters each. Unlike her each of us also had a baby.

We knew that our babies were boys because they wore trousers, knitted by Mama in pink. Pink, because she advocated freedom of choice and would not yield to the preju-

Feeding the ducks with Mama in the park

The four of us sat down with scissors, glue and old newspapers, and worked as gaily as if we were decorating the house for a birthday party.

dice that boys should wear blue. As a matter of fact, Mama adored the color blue. She used to buy blue dresses for us in a shop called *Baby House* and continued to order large sizes long after we had stopped being babies. She herself nearly always wore blue and she was so tiny that people who walked behind us while we paraded our toy strollers through the park of a Sunday, sometimes believed we were four sisters, playing, laughing and throwing bread crumbs to the ducks.

However, on Friday, May 10th, 1940, our merry little playmate of yesterday suddenly became an authority on matters of war. Had she not, at the outbreak of the First World War, fled from Antwerp to Amsterdam with a pillow case full of pots and pans thrown over her shoulder? Had she not seen buildings collapse and windows shatter? She declared that we should stick strips of adhesive tape to the windows. But since we didn't have any such tape, the four of us sat down with scissors, glue and old newspapers, and worked as gaily as if we were decorating the house for a birthday party.

Alkmaar

In our back-yard, just before Papa left

Around ten o'clock Papa phoned from Alkmaar where his regiment was stationed. "Paula," he said, "take a taxi and come here with the girls. I want to kiss you good-bye before I leave for the battle front."

He gave the address of a school in Alkmaar, and urged us to hurry.

Mama made one phone call after the other, but it wasn't easy to persuade a driver to take us to Alkmaar and back. Although the battle above our heads had quieted down after sunrise, no one knew if, when and where fights might break out, and if it would be possible to return to Amstelveen once we had left.

People preferred to stay home and close their doors. Some, who had a better place to go and the means to reach it, left maybe never to return. No one felt like cruising the country for the sake of some romantic soldier who wanted to kiss his wife and daughters good-bye.

When Mama finally found a driver who agreed to take us, he wanted so much money that we had to waste precious time driving from one acquaintance to another to borrow any sum they could spare.

Following Myriam's advice, Alexandra and I stuffed our pockets with handkerchiefs in case we needed to cry. In addition, Myriam carried an empty purse, and I a chamber pot for spitting, since I was recovering from the whooping cough. Poor Alexandra cried bitterly because she had not been able to think of some additional item to take with her.

Late that afternoon we reached Alkmaar and the school Papa had mentioned. He stood by the gate, worried lest we wouldn't come. We fell into his arms, and the five of us became one big, hugging, kissing human knot.

After a while our driver reminded us that he wanted to return to his own family and that we'd better get into his cab again.

But our tall Papa and our tiny Mama would not be disentangled. Nor would they let go of us.

"Take the money and go," said one of the five heads of the human knot to the taxi driver. "We're staying together." Presently the roll call for the soldiers was sounded. Papa drew the various parts of his body together and jumped over the fence. Swinging his long legs and adjusting his khaki cap on his newly cropped head, he disappeared behind the school building. The four of us huddled together and waited.

"If ever there was a time to light Shabbos candles," said Mama, "it would be now." She didn't explain the meaning of the word Shabbos. Neither did she light any candles.
Before long, Papa returned with wonderful news. His regiment would not travel East during the night as scheduled. Mama cried silently. Was it from happiness because of the unexpected delay, or from worry because she didn't know where we would spend the night?

The Nunnery

Papa was a wizard. He could guess how many matches were in a box and recite the alphabet backwards. On birthday parties he used to delight our guests by transforming eggs into Ping-Pong balls and Ping-Pong balls into eggs. Now, seeing that we were cold and tired, he announced that he would forthwith hocus-pocus us into a nice warm bedroom if we stopped worrying.

A nunnery bordered on the school where Papa's

Papa asking the nun for help for his family

regiment was billeted. Although the shutters were closed for the night, Papa rang the bell. An old nun peeped through a tiny hole in the door. Papa smiled. The nun unbolted the door and the two of them talked.

After a few minutes, the nun led us through a long corridor into a room with two beds. The four of us lay down, two to a bed, and the old nun patiently waited in the doorway while Papa drew the blankets over his four little women and kissed us good night, starting with Alexandra who was the youngest, and lingering with Mama as long as he dared.

Papa expected to be sent to the war front any day, so we stayed in the nunnery. During air raids we were summoned to the communal hall where the nuns recited as many *Ave Maria's* as there were beads on their rosaries. The Mother Superior suggested that we join the nuns in prayer, but Mama whispered in our ears that we shouldn't, because we didn't believe in Jesus (who hang on a large wooden cross above our heads), but that this was a secret, and that we should, therefore, close our eyes, fold our hands, and move our lips while thinking hard of something else.

"Think of what, Mama?"

"Whatever you like. Invent a fairy tale."

On Tuesday evening Papa received permission to enter our room for a final farewell. His regiment was leaving, and he himself would drive the bus. Not that he had ever driven a bus, but the other soldiers didn't even know how to drive an ordinary car.

Mama, who otherwise never let us out of sight, asked a novice to keep an eye on us and disappeared to see Papa off. After midnight she woke us up, crying with joy. The Dutch army had surrendered. Papa would never leave us. As far as my sisters and I were concerned, the war was over.

A Jewish tortoise

Papa had to stay in Alkmaar until after demobilization, but the four of us returned to Amstelveen. Mama used to accompany us to and from school for fear we would wander off to pick buttercups and marigolds in the endless stretches of tall grass where red cows stood dozing in the sun. Or else we might linger on the dike and fall into the canal, that mysterious black water of my childhood, where dredgers in oilskin clothes used to load tons of evil-smelling mud on flat barges. From where did all that mud come and where did it go? Each time I asked Mama, she told me to run along because of the stench. But I, like Lot's wife whom I knew from our Illustrated Children's Bible, turned around and inhaled the sharp smell of decay.

One day I took my tortoise Zarathustra to school. Next day Lotte, who was the princess of the class, brought her tortoise, too. I had no idea that Zarathustra was Jewish until Lotte explained it to me.
"If you have two marbles or two tortoises or two flowers, the one that looks different is Jewish."

We compared our tortoises scrupulously, and although I agreed with Lotte that they were not identical, I found it hard to tell which of the two was the Jew.

"How can you know?" I asked Lotte.

"Ask Jesus," she said.

I was shocked. "My mother says that we don't believe in him."

"What? Don't you have a tree in the house for his birthday, when Father Christmas comes with all the presents? But then you must be Jewish yourself. That's terrible!"

We went to the toilets and compared our faces in the mirror.

"There you are," said Lotte. She wrinkled her nose and touched its tip with her index finger. "You look different. You are a Jew."

Sunday School

I waited until Papa had returned from Alkmaar before throwing my newly obtained wisdom in the middle of the dining table. "Myriam is a Jew!" I blurted out.

Papa and Mama laid down their forks, looked at each other, and talked German. There was nothing my sisters and I hated more than when our parents conversed in their secret language. To show that I knew what it was all about, I wrinkled my nose, touched its tip with my index finger, and announced, "Lotte says that the one who looks different is the Jew. Alexandra and I wear our hair in cork-screws, but Myriam's hair is frizzy. And she wears spectacles. So she is the Jew. If you don't believe me, ask Jesus!"

"Look here," Papa burst out, "there's no difference between Jews and non-Jews. There can only be a difference between good and bad people."

"And don't start Jesusing me in my own house," Mama added in a voice so calm that it could only predict a storm.

"I'm not Jesusing you," I protested "I'm only saying that we'd better buy a tree for him when he has his birthday. Otherwise we may soon all become Jews wheth-er we like it or not."

"It's true," said Papa. "To avoid suspicion, we should sent the girls to Sunday school. And we should also stop speaking French in the street."

It was then that we learned that our Mama was a Jew, which was perfectly legitimate, were it not that the Germans might kill her if they found out. As the Germans were temporarily lording it over the Netherlands, we would be allowed to attend Sunday school just like everybody else.

"But," said Mama, "promise not to believe what the parson tells you."

The parson was a lady called Mrs Modderman. She composed songs and accompanied herself on the lute. She told us about Little Lord Jesus and gave us snap-shots of him. I had one snapshot on which he looked like my baby doll, Robbie, and another on which he figured, wrapped in a cloak of golden hair, and resembled Lotte with whom I soon was in fierce competition for the title of most zealous pupil in Sunday school.

On the bicycle to The Hague

All of a sudden the Germans ordered the Jews to sew a yellow star on their clothes. Mama, who wore such a star, said that there was no point for us to continue attending Sunday school, now that everybody knew our secret, but Papa said that we could stay, since he intended to un-star Mama by de-Jewing her.

Papa used to wear a long leather coat. I hated that coat because it felt like an iron fence between our bodies when he hugged me good-bye before leaving home in the morning.

Years later we learned that he didn't always go to his office, but often rode on his bike without tires all the way from Amsterdam to The Hague, and that he did not only wear his leather coat against the piercing wind, but also because he wanted to pose as a collaborator with the Germans, among whom leather coats were fashionable.

Sporting his leather coat and a matching cap, he greeted his so-called fellow collaborators in The Hague with the party cry *'Houzee'* and the German guards of Seyss-Inquart's headquarters with *'Heil Hitler'*.

Papa on his bicycle. .

"Houzee!"

What did he do at headquarters? Nothing much, except use the toilets, buy a German newspaper or a cup or substitute coffee in the mess room, converse in fluent German with officers who happened to hang around there, curse the weather and those damned Jews, or discuss the gratification of self-sacrifice for 'Our Beloved Fuhrer'. He shared cigarettes he had bought on the black market and became a familiar character around the premises. Nobody knew what his job was, but no one doubted that it was important.

Jewish or not Jewish?

One night the Germans rounded up Mama's mother, sister and aunt. Papa rushed to the notorious *Hollandsche Schouwburg* where the three ladies were temporarily interned, and succeeded in a last-minute now-or-never effort to persuade the Germans they were making a fatal error.

Old Mrs Horowitz, he claimed, was a Catholic, who had been expelled from Belgium to Holland at the outbreak of the First World War because her husband held an Austrian passport. Apparently, in the confusion she had been registered as a Jew without being aware of it.

"Of course, we are much indebted to you for ridding our country of the Jews," Papa told the Germans. "Only don't overdo it. You might kill an Aryan and that would be murder."

If what Papa claimed to be the truth about my grandmother could be proven, the Horowitz siblings might be promoted to the blessed state of half-Jews, which at that time still equaled the verdict 'non-guilty'.

Old Mrs Horowitz and her daughter were allowed to live at home until their case would be investigated. To give his argument weight, Papa relied on some German pseudo-scientists who had written popular books in which they argued that the inferiority of Jewish souls was reflected in their physical traits.

Emmy Andriesse took pictures of Mama under conditions that made her look taller and blonder than she actually was.

"Judge for yourself," said Papa to the Germans in the Hague. "Can this lady have more than fifty percent of Jewish blood in her veins?"

The result of Papa's ruse was that Mama unstitched the yellow star she had worn on the lapel of her coat, and never stitched it on again.

The only relative who tragically slipped through the mazes of Papa's prevarications was my grandfather's sister Zeena, the widow of the one-time sugar magnate and millionaire, the well-known German Jew, David Zaitsoff.

Great-Aunt Zeena was a very unhappy lady who had never loved her husband. During the Russian revolution the couple fled from Kiev to Berlin with their daughter Helena and their son Solomon. Solomon died of consumption when still a very young man. When Helena subsequently fell in love with a gentile, her father threatened to commit suicide if she married him. Helena gave in to her father's intimidations, but swore to punish him by never getting married, thus denying him progeny. She returned to Russia, became a Bolshevik *commisar* and severed all ties with her parents.

"I could not keep my son alive," Great-Aunt Zeena used

to sigh. "And I could not let my daughter live."

I will never forget Papa's haggard face when he filled a knapsack with a woolen blanket and the old tin utensils he had used as a boy scout, and went to see our eighty-one-year-old great-aunt off at the railway station of Amsterdam.

The files in Yad Vashem record the grand old lady died in Auschwitz on February 12th, 1943. According to eye-witnesses she died already in the train that was to bring her there.

Papa had a special bond with Great-Aunt Zeena

Fooling the Nazi's

Papa's failure to save my mother's aunt had badly shaken his self-confidence, but he did not have the time to mourn one Jew while so many others needed his help.

The more Jews Papa un-starred, the more sophisticated were the games he played. At the time he told no one what he was doing, and after the war we got to know only some of his pranks, such as the one he staged for Emmy Andriesse.

Pretending to need a medical check-up, he visited an old doctor who, being himself of German origin, was as pedantic and meticulous as the enemy himself. They talked about the war, the weather and the good old times when people still had a professional conscience.

In an atmosphere, carefully packed with nostalgia, Papa asked, "Do you really never throw away old files?"

The doctor stuck his thumbs in his armpits and proudly answered, "Come and see!" He took Papa down to the cellar and said, "Here are the records of every single patient who has ever consulted me. But who gives a straw for history, nowadays? Soon my life's work will end up on the rubbish dump just like everything else in this accursed country."

Papa admired the neatly bound files, paid for his consultation, and went home with in his briefcase a tome, carefully selected for the date on its binding.

In those days people paid for the gas in their cooking stoves by sliding coins in a slot machine. Each family had such a gas meter in the cellar. A few days after Papa's visit to the doctor, he returned, this time disguised as the gas coin collector, and restored the kidnapped tome to its place on the shelf. On the appropriate page he had inserted in faded blue ink in the doctor's handwriting that Emmy's father had, as a result of the mumps, lost his virility.

However, to prove that old Mr Andriesse could not possibly be Emmy's father was only half the game. The next step was to prove that her so-called real father was an Aryan. With this in mind Papa stole the old files of an obscure little hotel in Venlo, and inserted the names of two guests who apparently had rented a double room nine months before Emmy was born, some forty years earlier. The guests were Emmy's mother and a man whose resounding surname left no doubt as to his Aryan pedigree.

How did the Germans discover these forged papers? Papa never told us or, if he did, I must have forgotten.

Did someone drop them a hint as to the ancient adultery scheme? Did the Germans, maybe even in Papa's charming company, laugh their heads off at the expense of that dirty Jew, Emmy's father, who had been cuckolded by a smart full-blooded Aryan? Like my readers, I am left wondering....

After the war Papa would answer this kind of questions with a shrug and say, "Not all the Germans were natural murderers. Some of them would rather keep their hands clean than kill a human being. But everything had to look as genuine as possible and the most important rule of the game for both opponents was keeping a poker face."

Uncle Arie de Froe

From the day Mama had officially become an Aryan, our home became a shelter for less fortunate Jews. More often than not we ate breakfast with guests who had come overnight. Whether they were old men, widows, young girls, spinsters, people we knew from sight or people we had never met before, they never had any names other than Aunt or Uncle.

Only one of our regular guests was not a Jew. He was Uncle Arie De Froe, a big and rather phlegmatic man with a broad grin. Uncle Arie and Papa used to spend long nights jotting down figures and drawing up tabulations of what they called 'characteristics of the Jews'.

Uncle Arie de Froe

Uncle Arie often slept in the study, and we were sometimes allowed to admire his fascinating collection of false dentures, tufts of hair and glass eyes. He was forever pursuing whoever slept under our roof with various rulers, which he bent in all directions in order to measure the most unlikely curves of the human body.

Jews, it appeared, had formerly been recognized by their crooked noses. This, Uncle Arie claimed, was not scientific. It became necessary to measure the distance between their eyes, and to compare the shade of their nails with complicated color charts.

There were numbers to indicate the maximum and minimum length of Jewish ears, eyelashes and toes.

The book *Rasse und Seele* was published in Germany before the Second World War. In it the author explains the physical differences between inferior peoples, such as Jews and Gypsies, and the Aryan superman. This is the kind of popular books on which Uncle Arie based his 'research'.

In order to classify a person as a Jew, one had to take into account the shade of his teeth, and determine the number of pores per square centimeter of his skin, the distance between his navel and his chin, between the nape of his neck and the tip of his tail bone, and to compare everything with everything else. The method was trustworthy and systematic.

The Germans couldn't have wished for anything more convincing. Although my sisters and I did not always know what Uncle Arie was trying to prove, we were quick to discover that whatever the outcome of his calculations, they always culminated in Papa donning his leather coat and straddling his bicycle.

"Look at the case of Mr So-and-so," he would say to the Germans in The Hague. "According to the anthropologic findings of Doctor De Froe, Mr So-and-so cannot possibly have more than twelve-and-a-half percent of Jewish blood. Don't you think you should investigate?"

And the Germans were only too happy to oblige. As long as they were busy sifting the Jews from the Aryans, they could justify their stay in Holland where their lives were safe and their stomachs filled. When there would be no more work for them in Holland, they would be sent to the east front where they would surely perish.

So they searched for evidence, raided hospitals and warehouses for old files, and appointed additional manpower to translate and decipher everything ever written about Mr So-and-so and his family tree, true or false. Indeed, the more riddles they solved, the more they became convinced that people who had quietly been posing as Jews, actually carried vast quantities of superior Aryan blood in their veins. For the Germans in the Netherlands Uncle Arie was an authority and Papa a necessity.

Hiding Place

Although Papa always tried to find safer addresses for his Jews than what he himself could offer, he sometimes had so many of them under his care that some had to live in our attic, at least temporarily. We urgently needed a hide-out.

To plan a double wall in the attic was one thing, to build it, another. How could we smuggle fourteen square meters of bricks into the house without attracting the atten-tion of our neighbors? Our wizard knew the answer. Twice a day, three innocent little girls walked home from school. Twice a day we playfully made a little detour through the park to pick flowers. Twice a day we each stumbled, quite unex-pectedly, on a nice red brick, carefully dropped between the dead leaves under the rose bushes. We never hid bricks in our school bags if a stranger happened to stroll in the neighborhood. We never met the mysterious brick provid-er. I don't know if other brick carriers of any sex, age or creed shared our job, or how mortar was smuggled into our house, as well as the long wooden boards that eventually became a cupboard to hide the entrance to our secret shel-ter. What I do know is that in front of the newly built cupboard, between the floor of the attic and the ceiling of our bedroom, a second hide-out was built. The trap door to this one was invisible enough to be convincing, but visible enough to be discovered. In this second-best shelter Papa kept chocolate bars, cigarettes and cognac to soften the stomachs of possible finders. There he also kept papers, forged especially with a view to sending the enemy on time-consuming dead-end tracks.

Jesus

One afternoon I cribbed in class and had to stand in the corner for twenty minutes after school. It thus happened that I strolled along the dike on my way home without my sisters. The fields were flooded, the cows were eaten up by the Germans, the dredgers in oilskin clothes were either dead or digging trenches in Germany. Two men were crossing the bridge. One of them collapsed without a word. The other, a German soldier, turned him over with his boot, mumbled *"Tot,"* and continued on his way.

I waited a few minutes and went to look at the dead man. On his lapel was a yellow star. I knew that I should not linger by the bridge lest the German return and ask me

As I was squatting under a bush to grope for my brick, a ray of the setting sun fell on my hand.

questions, but I thought I might offer the dead man a small sign of my sympathy. I searched my pockets and found half a slice of dry bread that I had kept for later. I placed it on the yellow star and ran away as fast as I could. When I reached the end of the dike, I turned around as usual.

A gull was pecking at the bread on the dead man's breast. The German stood on the bridge. He lifted his rifle, aimed at the gull and missed. The bird flew up and circled above the dike, screaming a heart-rending "Jew! Jew…"

As usual, I walked home through the park. As I was squatting under a bush to grope for my brick, a ray of the setting sun fell on my hand. I looked up to see where it came from and saw, standing on a bough, shining red and golden between the flaming autumn leaves, Jesus. He was even more handsome than on the snapshots I kept under my pil-low. He wore his embroidered dress and stretched both arms high in front, palms down, as if saluting *Heil Hitler* with double intensity.

"You are the bravest girl I know, "said Jesus, and golden drops rained from his fingertips. His voice sounded as sweet as Mrs Modderman's lute. "You gave your bread to the dead man on the dike and you are not afraid to be alone in the park and carry a brick for your secret shelter."

Immediately I became afraid, but Jesus continued, "I have chosen you to proclaim among the Jews that there is a solution to their problems. It is no longer necessary for the Jews to hide. If they all believe in me, they won't have to wear yellow stars on their lapels and then the Germans will no longer know the difference between Jews and ordinary people. Go into the world and spread the word: A king has been born unto you."

I didn't particularly like the sentence about the king because it sounded like bragging. On the other hand even Papa didn't know how to save all the Jews at one blow. Someone who did know might well be forgiven for boasting about it, and generally speaking Jesus was right: to proclaim a few sentences was more practical than to carry bricks. The problem was, I didn't want Mama to know that I had been listening to the flatteries of a stranger. Having cribbed in school was trouble enough. Moreover, would Mama believe what Jesus had said if she did not even believe that he existed? Should I tell Mrs Modderman? She, at least, didn't have to be convinced that the Lord, as she called him, was capable of balancing himself on a bough.
She even believed that he could revive the dead, although she had never seen him do it. But what if she asked why I

had been all alone in the park at sunset? One thing was more important than everything else: not to betray the secret of our nearly finished hide-out for the aunts and uncles who lived upstairs.

Without telling anybody what bothered me, I made various plans to help Jesus carry out his project, but dropped them all. However, Jesus kept appearing, sometimes in the bedroom when Myriam and Alexandra were asleep, sometimes in broad daylight, perched on the edge of a cloud or on the kitchen slab.

As weeks went by and I didn't fulfill his expectations, I thought he would become angry, but he was only sad. "Time is working against you," he reminded me with a mournful smile. "The longer you wait, the more Jews will be killed by the Germans." Although he didn't say so, I knew that I deserved to be burned at the stake like Joan of Arc, whose portrait Mrs Modderman had shown us. When nobody punished me, I decided to do it myself by offering my precious collection of snapshots to Lotte with whom my love-hate relationship had reached an all-time peak. Before I had properly explained why I wanted to give them to her, she had already snapped them out of my hand and put them safely between the pages of her bible. Narrowing her eyes like a viper, she spit her poison in my ear. "I know why you don't want them. You are a Jew. I told you so."

Christmas Party

I didn't sleep. I didn't eat. I tried to conjure up Jesus by kneeling on my bare knees on the icy bathroom tiles while fingering a string of beads like the nuns in Alkmaar had done. In vain. When winter set in, I became terrified by the idea that the Germans had planted Lotte in Sunday school so she could spy on me, and that she would bring about the downfall of my family and our hidden Jews. To counteract her evil schemes, I demanded that we have a Christmas party.

Mama said "No". I did not stamp my foot. I did not raise my voice. I simply asserted my rights as a Jew, a Christian and a human being, and made it known in Sunday school that I had met Father Christmas and that he had promised presents for all the girls who would come to a Christmas party in our home. I also Invited Mrs Modderman. She declined, but agreed to lend me her book with the musical notes of our favorite Christmas carols, so I could enliven the party with my violin. I spent hours practicing 'Silent night, holy night', preferably by the open window for the benefit of our neighbors. The Jews who lived in our house complained that I hurt their ears. The more they complained, the louder I practiced and the stronger I relished the fact that I was going to rescue them from treason by luring the very traitor into the conspirator's den. Neither Lotte nor anyone would suspect that only one ceiling away from us, Jews so genuine that even Papa could not de-Jew them, were keeping their breath under penalty of death. I even devised a game which included bumping on that very ceiling with a broomstick. While upstairs the tension would become unbearable, Lotte would receive her Christmas present out of my hands. For since we all had outgrown the fairy tale of Father Christmas, I would appear in his stead, wrapped in Papa's purple dressing gown, with a cotton-wool beard and, for a hat, Mama's checkered tea cozy.

I had promised that Father Christmas would give a present to each of my guests. Since twelve girls had accepted my invitation and I could not leave my sisters and parents out, that added up to sixteen presents. To be as good as my word, I fell into a creative spell. I spent all my pocket money on colored threads, paint and beads, inasmuch as such luxuries were still available. Every afternoon I rushed through my homework and secluded myself in Papa's study. I glued postcards on plywood and sawed them into puzzles.

I drilled tiny holes in seashells and strung them to necklaces. I drew sets of greeting cards and embroidered initials on used but still passable handkerchiefs. Sometimes Papa appeared in his study and gave me a hand. He didn't ask questions but simply showed me a better way to hold the drill or helped me steer the jigsaw. When I broke my last fret saw, he gave me a quarter to buy a whole new bunch. I consulted him about entertainment, too. As there were no eggs, he would not be able to perform the trick with the Ping-Pong balls, but he promised to guess the number of matches in a box, and helped me compose a long Christmas poem which I would recite while distributing the gifts.

The most difficult problem was how to get a Christmas tree. Mama wouldn't have anything to do with it. As usual, Papa came to my rescue. He gave me money for a medium-sized bough. He also helped me nail it upright to a wooden box. It cut quite a figure as it stood in the corner of our living room. Myriam, who sided with Mama, turned her back on it, but Alexandra helped me cut, draw, glue and fold paper decorations. We constructed a star of Bethlehem out of iron wire, and a cross out of two pencils tied together with a piece of string. When Mama understood that no one short of Hitler would be able to cancel my party, she cooked rose hip jam to serve with the substitute tea, but only on the condition that I remove the cross. I was only too happy to agree. I did not really like it myself.

Our crib, on the other hand, was out of this world. I dressed up my doll Marguerite as the Virgin Mary and made her stand upright between a plush elephant and squirrel who figured as the ass and oxen. Joseph and the shepherds were represented by a woolen monkey and three rag dolls. Other toy animals were the three Kings.

My baby doll, Robbie, cast for the Savior in that magical moment when he actually descends from heaven, dangled from our would-be tree above a manger which in itself was a miracle of daring ingenuity. To build it, we had used four bricks that had been left unused after our own holiest of holies, the best hiding place in the world, was completed. Even Mama could not suppress a smile when she saw it.

Finally, the great day came. Everything went according to plan. My only regret was that Papa banned our Jews to the attic so that my broomstick game became senseless.

But crowding in the attic did not prevent the Jews from having to suspend their eternal quarrels for the duration of my party. They stood the challenge heroically. On the whole, I was in complete control of every detail except one: during all these hectic weeks I had never stopped believing that Jesus would have the grace to show up at his birthday party and admit that I was not a total failure. I had rehearsed a hundred times how I would humbly advise him to release me from my duty and employ Lotte instead. But Jesus never appeared to me again. Although I was thoroughly vexed, I was also relieved.

Years later I had a similar experience when a suitor I had planned to sack, deprived me of a chance to do so by sacking me first.

More tortoises

Our house on 25 Rodenburghlaan, Amstelveen, was wedged between two similar houses. We had a small front garden in which Mama forbade us to play for fear we would pick up dirty words from street urchins, and a long, narrow back garden in which my sisters and I each had our personal plot of approximately one square meter. Being the middle daughter, I had the middle plot. Sometimes Mama allowed me to roam the neighborhood, equipped with a tin bucket and a discarded tablespoon to rescue unsightly plants from between the paving stones where pedestrians might trample them. I had a great affection for these brave outcasts, and carefully transferred them to my personal plot where they could grow and flower to their heart's desire.

My sisters were less interested in gardening. Alexandra was still too young and Myriam preferred books. Seeing that my sisters did not tend their plots, Mama bought a paper bag full of Indian cress seeds and let them scatter it around. In no time the bright orange flowers rampaged all over the place and I had to face the one dilemma that lies at the root of most man-made catastrophes: to go to war against the Indian cress, or allow the strong to destroy the vulnerable.

Fighting for the rights of my weeds included keeping the tortoises off the premises. Since we were against keeping animals in a cage, I had to watch their every movement, and the more I watched them, the more I came to love them, too. When our very smallest tortoise, Rabindranath Tagore, disappeared, I was so sad that Mama put an ad in the local newspaper. Instantly we were rewarded by a deluge of tortoises, acquired in the local animal store by various people who were not at all sorry to get rid of them, now that the war compelled them to grow string beans and potatoes in their gardens for survival. Accordingly, our household was enriched with Homerus, Reaumur, Michelangelo, Penelope and many others whose names have slipped from my memory.

Soon we had more tortoises in our garden than Jews in our attic. The tortoises accommodated themselves with grass and leaves, but the Jews needed something more substantial to eat. Many householders would readily have harbored a Jew or two if only they had come with a beefsteak attached to their lapels instead of a yellow star. For them Jews and food were a package deal.

Papa, who suffered from a surplus of Jews and a deficit of food, needed a great deal of money to balance the scales. Where could he find help? He went to his father.

Grandfather Dirk van Hulst

Opa Dirk van Hulst

Mama openly disliked her in-laws. She claimed that they had not wanted the object of their adoration to marry a Jew. However, Papa maintained that, very early in his relationship with Mama, his father had whispered in his ear, "Congratulations, son. I wish I had had the guts to marry a peppercorn like yours."

And indeed, Mama was no bore. Apart from being musical and artistic, she had a great talent for imitating people. Papa's mother and two unmarried sisters belonged to her favorite targets. Her after dinner performances used to culminate in orgies of laughter during which the five of us rolled over the floor, gasping for breath. Although these spells of hilarity forged an unbreakable bond between us, I used to wonder why Papa did not stop Mama from making his family ridiculous, especially since he had a very special brand of humor himself. One day, for instance, he went for a walk in the snow, barefoot, swinging a walking stick like Charlie Chaplin, and donning his dressing gown and top hat for no other reason than to make us laugh.

Another day, when Mama had asked him to rasp cheese for a spaghetti dish she was preparing in the kitchen, he cut the two-pound piece of cheese into beadlike cubes which he threaded with a darning needle. He hung the string on the lamp and ate it, first lying flat on his back on the floor and ending up tiptoeing between the plates on the dining table.

Whether or not my gentile grandparents approved of Papa's marriage to a Jewess I cannot tell, but I daresay that they were decent people who knew the difference between right and wrong. When Opa Dirk realized why Papa needed so much money, he gave him a third of his considerable fortune, which equaled Papa's future inheritance. However, to feed his Jews Papa needed more than money alone. He also needed a never-ending resourcefulness.

"The sky is the limit," he used to decree, and indeed the tricks he invented defied imagination.

Papa eating the cheese cubes

He discovered a modest sausage factory in the heart of Amsterdam and established contact with the man whose task it was to store away the daily output before the night shift took the floor. This man used to string some twenty to thirty sausages, each tied into a fat, succulent loop, on a pole which he swung over his shoulder, in the same way a tramp carries his bundle, at least in picture books. Two German guards were attached to this man; one watched him load up in the factory proper, the other watched him unload in the warehouse at the other end of the building. Neither of these guards had been instructed to accompany the sausage carrier on his way. Thus the man ran to and fro, to and fro, only slowing down ever so little before turning around a certain corner where a tiny skylight happened to be in the wall. This skylight faced an empty lot where one of Papa's trustees had dumped a truckload of gravel.

Every evening the sausage carrier would turn around that corner, take one step forward and two steps backwards, thus pushing the tip of his pole through the skylight for the fraction of a second. Whoever of Papa's trustees was hiding behind the mound of gravel would come home that evening with one, sometimes two sausages.

Uncles and Aunts

Uncles and aunts replaced each other like the days of the week. We always slept when it happened. Our very first aunt in hiding was Harry Romp's divorced wife, Lou. We had never suspected that she, too, was Jewish.

One uncle performed tricks with a penknife; another taught us to solve crossword puzzles; a third read us fairy tales; a fourth told us jokes. We liked them all, but none stayed longer than a few days.

There were children too, such as our four-year-old cousin Anneke van Dam who slept one night in Alexandra's bed and wailed for hours. We thought she cried for her mother, but all she wanted was a yellow star on her dress like the one her brothers, Hans and Eric, had worn when the Germans came for them. Hans used to sit in front of me in class. One day he did not come to school. I never saw him again. But Anneke survived the war. Today she has a daughter whose name is Chaya, the Hebrew word for 'being alive'.

And then there was Haym Elte, the only son of Mama's friend Rasha Rivlin. Haym's forged papers were so reliable that he didn't have to hide. His false name was Hein. He was fifteen, posed as an apprentice in the carpenter's workshop behind Papa's office, and lunched with us every day.

One summer afternoon our neighborhood committee organized street contests. Hein, cocksure and magnificent, proposed to run the fifty meters with me on his shoulders. Before I knew what was happening, I held on to his head, and clasped his muscular neck between my bare legs.

While he galloped through the street like a wild stallion, the harsh smell of his sweat rose to my nostrils and his blood pulsed between my thighs. I screamed a long bewildered scream, but Hein had no time to pay attention to his

Myriam, Hans van Dam, Hannah, Alexandra

rider. He sprinted on, sweating, pulsing, yelling, never stopping until he fell down, exhausted, at the finish, and I had my first full-blown orgasm.

Reliable and Unreliable Neighbors

Our neighbors on number 27 collaborated with the Germans, but our neighbors on number 23, the Johansens, were OK. One night somebody rang their bell. When Miep Johansen opened the door, she found a newborn baby on the doorstep. She took him in and called him Benny after her husband, whose name was Bernhard, like that of our Prince Consort.

After the war, the contact person who was supposed

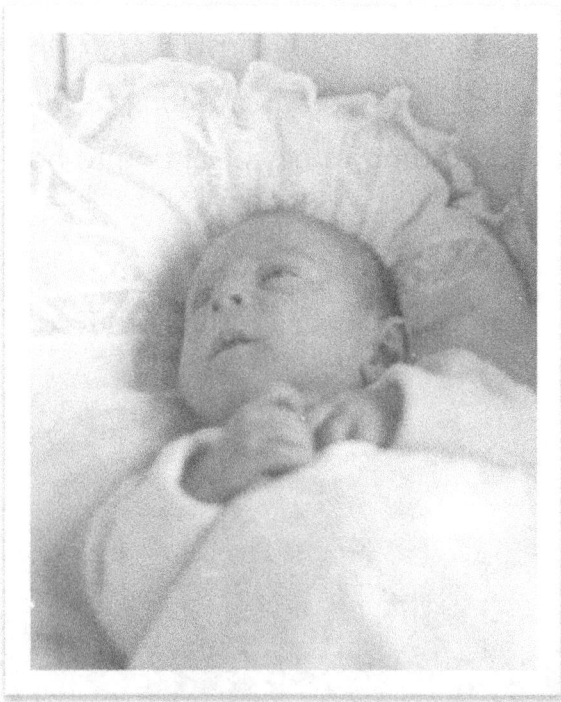

A newborn baby on the doorstep

to know Benny's identity failed to appear. Miep and Ben Johansen, who had no other children, had good reasons to hope that nobody would ever come for Benny who was, by then, a doll of a toddler.

One Sunday, when Ben and Benny Johansen were on their way home from church, an unknown young woman stopped them and said, "What a nice grandson you have."

"He is not my grandson," answered the proud father. "He is my son!"

"Is that so?" the woman continued. "At your age, such a young child…. I was wondering…. Indeed, I was struck by his likeness with my daughter Maud…. He couldn't be an adopted child, by any chance? A Jewish child? He couldn't be my lost son?"

Benny returned to his Jewish mother and sister. A few days later Ben Johansen died of heart failure. Benny's father, whose name was Benjamin Hazan, had been killed by the Germans. The mother could not have given her son a more appropriate name than the one he already had. So Benny he was and Benny he remained. And it was Benny's mother who revealed to us that the vanished contact person had been our own Mama who was, by then, no longer alive.

This little story serves to illustrate how careful people were not to involve even their closest partners in underground affairs. After all, the less you knew, the less you could tell if you were caught.

Rudy Reisel

The Johansens also lodged Rudy Reissel. Of course my sisters and I never met Rudy until after the war when he was already a strapping young man in his early twenties. By that time we were three giggling teenagers who fell collectively in love with him, but he went on *aliyah* and our hearts were not broken.

Before Rudy left the Netherlands, he told us that he had been in hiding in Amsterdam for some time, when he learned that the Germans had caught his contact person. Clearly the address where he lived was no longer safe. His hostess confided in a friend who promised to see what he could do. The matter was urgent. That same evening, after curfew, a member of the Gestapo came for Rudy.

"This is the end," poor Rudy thought.

But the stranger murmured in Dutch, "Don't fear. I have

come to take you to a safer place. Jump onto my luggage carrier."

Although Rudy had never met Papa, he had no choice but to do as he was told. Papa sprinted away as fast as his bike with wooden tires would carry him. At the outskirts of Amsterdam they ran into a German barricade. In the pitch dark Papa doubled his speed.

A watchman called in German, "Who goes there?"

Papa retorted in unfaltering German, *"Ich bin's*! It's me!" And on he sped with Rudy on his carrier. It was long past mid-night when he delivered the trembling young man at Parson Schouten's home in Amstelveen.

Parson Schouten was a devout Christian, who considered it his holy duty to bring the Jews to reason. Parson Schouten also considered himself a sensible man. When he saw that the Jew he had so charitably taken into his home put up a strong resistance against the church, he said, "I'll give you six months to make up your mind. Here is my library. Use it freely."

Rudy, who didn't have anything else to do, spent the best part of his days with Parson Schouten's learned, theological tomes. After six months Parson Schouten requested an answer to the question whether Rudy did or did not believe in Jesus Christ. Rudy said "No!"

"In that case," said Parson Schouten, "you must leave my house at once. You are endangering my soul before the Lord."

It was then that Papa brought Rudy to Ben and Miep Johansen where he stayed until the end of the war.

The Three who Remained

Of all the Jews who spent one or more nights in our house, three stayed on. Ann Petersen, whom Mama treated like a daughter, lived with us for two or three years.

Mama used to say, "After the war, Ann will marry out of our house." But after the war Mama was dead and Ann, who emerged as Vera Cohen, immigrated to South Africa. We never heard from her again.

Uncle Frits and Aunt Kitty also remained. Uncle Frits was a violinist without a violin, a former student of Mama's venerated teacher, Alexander Schmuller. Mama admired Uncle Frits so much that she lent him her own expensive violin and borrowed a simpler instrument for herself. Every evening after the curtains were drawn, Uncle Frits tiptoed

Uncle Frits playing a duet with Mama.

downstairs to play duets with Mama. Our unreliable neighbors, who lived on the other side of our living room wall, couldn't tell the difference between the sound of one or two violins, but seemed to hate music as a way of life, and often pounced on the wall to remind us of it.

Sometimes I woke up in the night while Mama and Uncle Frits were playing. The music made me feel as if I were an egg on the verge of hatching. On such nights I would slip out of bed and sit on the stairs, wrapped in my blanket. Sometimes the music stopped after a few pieces and I went back to bed before anyone discovered me. At other times Papa opened the door to the corridor, as if he knew I was sitting there, and called me in. Then I would climb on his knees and we would huddle together in a dark corner of the room, listen together, ache together, laugh and cry together. Laugh because we were privileged to hear and see, cry because we did not have the key to the musical tower of love Uncle Frits and Mama were building by the flickering light of a single carbide lamp, burning with the sour smell of witchcraft and thunderstorms.

Tortoises in a box

In the fall of 1944 we brought our tortoises to the cellar, where they would hibernate in a box filled with dry leaves. "I wish I were a tortoise," said Mama. "I wish I could sleep in a little box and wake up in a better world." A week later she fell ill. The name of her disease was *Colitis Ulcerosa*. She went to a hospital for an operation and promised to return home within a month. Ann, Uncle Frits and Aunt Kitty stayed in our house with Papa. Myriam moved in with the family Hendrikse around the corner but came home every day so that the neighbors wouldn't wonder when seeing or hearing movements in the house during the hours papa was out. Alexandra and I moved in with the family Mertens on the Machineweg. Although we were living through the worst winter of the Second World War, the time we spent with Aunt Ans and Uncle Her Mertens was one of the most creative periods of my life.

Uncle Her gave me one sheet of quarto paper a week. I used to cut every sheet into a big square and a small rectangle. From Mondays to Fridays I drew elaborated pictures on the small rectangles, saving the squares for the week-ends. On each square I illustrated a couplet of a naughty song Uncle Her used to teach us after dinner when we sat in the dark. For reasons I forgot I always gave these illus-tra-tions to Uncle Arie de Froe when he visited us with Papa.

Uncle Her had a large vegetable garden in which he also kept bees. When we had no more electricity, he made candles from bee wax. He used these candles sparingly. Every evening after the sun had set, and before Uncle Her lit one of his precious candles, I sat on the stairs and improvised on my violin while Alexandra and the two daughters of the house, Yessie and Eeneke, danced in the dark entrance hall.

Papa's main concern was still how to feed all the people in his care. At the outskirts of the municipality lived a farmer who had become rich by collaborating with the enemy. While the Germans had confiscated the livestock of most farmers long ago, Piet Fransen still had a stable full of milk cows. It was Rudy's idea to propose farmer Fransen a deal: If he delivered a certain pounds of potatoes and so-and-so many pints of milk a week without asking questions, Papa would testify in his favor after the war. Piet Fransen, who realized that the Germans were about to lose the war, and that he would have to pay for his evil deeds, agreed. After the war, Papa kept his promise.

School

Throughout the war, school was the only constant factor in our lives. Everything else stopped or changed or became forbidden without prior notice. Friends became enemies, Jews became Aryans or the other way round. People who had been alive yesterday were dead today. But when the Germans transformed our school into barracks for their own use, a gym was hired in which we continued to study as if our lives depended on two plus two is four. Since the gym could not contain more than sixty children at a time, two forms studied from eight to eleven in the morning, two others from eleven to two in the afternoon, and two from two to five in the evening. Every week the schedule changed. Myriam was already in high school. Alexandra and Yessie were in the same shift and could walk together, but Eeneke and I had to walk alone to and from school along that same spooky dike where I had once seen a man drop dead.

Since Mama was in hospital and could no longer give me violin lessons, Uncle Frits took care of that part of my education. Twice a week I took my violin with me to school and went to the Rodenburghlaan for a lesson before returning to Aunt Ans and Uncle Her. The lessons took place behind drawn curtains in Papa's study where Aunt Kitty used to light a tiny stove, and cook whatever dry beans or vegetables Papa had been able to obtain. After the music lesson I used to do my homework by the downstairs window so that the neighbors could see the house was inhabited. On one such day I saw a German soldier climb over the garden fence. At the same time someone banged on the front door. For years we had been drilled to cope with exactly this situation. For years Papa had expressed the hope that it would never happen, and I had wickedly counter-hoped it would. Not because I wanted something dreadful to happen to our Jews, but because I so desperately wanted to rescue them. And here, on January 29th, 1945, was my chance. All mine and only mine.

Misunderstanding

Before I describe what followed, I want to point out that years later a certain Tini Visser wrote a beautiful book about Amstelveen in war time, in which she mistakenly ascribed the greatest hour of my childhood to my sister Myriam. Myriam, who had been interviewed by Tini Visser, apologized to me for the inaccuracy. I know that people who read Tini Visser's book couldn't care less one way or the other, but I, who am writing this story for my children and grandchildren, want them to know that, unlike Lord Jim in Conrad's book of that name, I stood up to the challenge when it presented itself, and did not miss the chance of a lifetime to score goal. What happened on January 29th, 1945, has influenced my further life more than any single fact or event I can think of.

How it really happened

To say the truth, it was my body rather than my mind that handled the situation, for when I saw the German climb over the fence of our back garden, my muscles and bones reacted without consulting my brains. It was on their own initiative that my legs bounced to the kitchen and my hand turned the key to lock the rear entrance at the very moment the German was about to burst into the house.

"Open the door," he shouted in German.

"I can't!" I shouted back. "The lock is rusted. The key is stuck." I fumbled a little with the key, feigning to do my best and shouted, "Wait. Somebody is banging on the front door."

Following Papa's instructions to the letter, I lingered in the entrance hall, slipped my hand behind the coats on their hangers, and turned the light switch on and off, on and off, on and off. Not that we had either electricity or light bulbs, but that particular switch worked on a battery concocted by Papa and was connected to a buzzer in the leg of Uncle Frits and Aunt Kitty's bed.

Instead of answering the bell, I went back to the living room and sat down to a job pertaining exclusively to the last years of World War II: erasing yesterday's lessons out of my copybook in order to use the pages for today's homework. My rubber was as tiny as a collar button, but could not be exchanged for a new one in school before it was half its present size. Although my mind must have registered the persistent knocking on the front door, the only thing I remember is that I rubbed away at my homework until my heart stopped beating against my ribs like a wild sea against the rocks.

As in a dream, I saw myself pulling the strings of all the puppets in a macabre play. I knew what was happening in every corner of the house. My hands were working in the living room, but my mind watched the Jews being swallowed by the double wall in the attic, like dirty dishwater being sucked into the sink after I myself had lifted the plug. I erased words until all the Jews had become invisible. Only then did I pick up my school bag and saunter to the front door to open it. As if I were standing in front of a mirror, I saw myself, a cute little girl with braids and a copybook, smiling at the strangers, wondering what they wanted, inviting them to come in.

One of them was a German soldier. He ran to the kitchen door and turned the key to let his pal in. The other was a collaborator who questioned me in Dutch.

"Where is your father?"

"Don't know."

"Where is your mother?"

"In the hospital."

"Which hospital?"

"Don't know." I knew of course, but I wouldn't tell him. Just then I heard Myriam whistle our familiar tune in the street.

"Don't let her in," the German shouted, but I had already opened the door."

"OK, let her in, then, but don't let her out."

They ordered us upstairs. I casually carried my copybook in the hope that our uninvited guests would believe my thoughts were with my schoolwork.

"Who has lit this stove?" the collaborator asked.

"I did."

"Who has been cooking here?"

"Me."

"Why such a big pot? Are there any people in the house besides you?"

Myriam gestured that our guests were welcome to help themselves to the soup, but they turned up their noses at the watery mixture and locked us in Papa's study.

With her teeth Myriam tore the thread that held the pages of my copybook together. She selected two newly cleaned pages and, using soot from the stove, wrote one word on each. "Warn Papa."

We waited by the window until we saw our neighbor Johansen come home. We pounced on the glass pane at the risk of being heard by the Germans, and showed him the pages of my copybook. He nodded and walked away. The Germans burst into the room and asked what the noise was about. Myriam threw the pages into the stove and stirred the fire. The Germans left and locked us in again.

Alexandra

Mr Johansen, who had no idea how to warn Papa, was keeping watch at his window when, miraculously, Alexandra arrived. Mr Johansen called her in and told her about the message he had seen at our window. Alexandra, who was not yet ten years old, suggested that Papa might be visiting Mama in the hospital. Together they hurried to yet another neighborhood acquaintance whose phone was still in working order because he, like Papa, was a member of the fire brigade. From there Alexandra phoned the hospital and asked for Papa.

"He just left," said the person at the other end of the line.

"Please, "Alexandra cried out." It is terribly important! Run, call him back!"

Whoever had answered the phone did not ask unnecessary questions. She ran into the street, shouted after Papa and brought him back to the hospital to answer the lifesaving phone call.

"No," said Myriam." I'd rather talk Dutch."

Myriam

Myriam and I were still prisoners in the study when we heard the phone ring. The door swung open and the Germans ordered us to run downstairs where Myriam had to answer the phone while one of them pointed his gun at her. "Say everything is fine," the collaborator hissed, and he put his ear close to the receiver to hear who was at the other end of the line.

It was Papa, but instead of asking how Myriam was, or if he should come home, he proposed, "Shall we talk French, as we used to?"

"No, "said Myriam." I'd rather talk Dutch."

From this Papa concluded that somebody was threatening her. He continued to talk about this, that and the other, and closed the conversation without having tempted Myriam to endanger herself.

Aunt Kitty

In the meantime, elsewhere in the house an even greater drama was taking place. While sitting quietly in her dark hiding place, Aunt Kitty suddenly remembered that Papa had given her a great responsibility. "If ever the Germans come to our house," he had said, "take this leather bag with you behind the double wall. In it are the only incriminating papers I have. I entrust them to you, Kitty!"

Poor Aunt Kitty! In the commotion she had forgotten the leather bag on the stairs leading up to the attic and she could not even fathom how many lives were threatened by her neglect. Brave Aunt Kitty! When she heard the Germans go downstairs to answer the phone, she crept out of her hiding place and rescued the leather bag.

All is well that ends well

After the telephone conversation with Papa, the Germans locked us up in the study again and started searching the house. There was nothing we could do but listen to their footsteps and hope that our hidden Jews would not stir or sneeze in their hiding place.

Later we learned that the Germans had not been searching for Jews but for the radio transmitter Papa had rescued that very morning out of Harry Romp's house, after Harry, who used to broadcast to England, had been caught.

Suddenly the Germans roared like cannibals who had caught a missionary. Our hearts sank for the sake of Uncle Frits, Aunt Kitty and Ann. The door flew open and in marched two cannibals, triumphantly carrying their prey, which consisted of a carton of cigarettes and a bottle of cognac they had found in the second-best hiding place, the one Papa had built with the intention that it would be discovered. A moment later the third cannibal came in with our box full of hibernating tortoises and a long kitchen knife. Singing nostalgic songs he set himself to scrubbing and cutting his catch. Without winking an eye they added Oedipus Rex, Fahrenheit and the others to the scanty soup which was still sputtering on the stove. When dinner was ready, they invited us to share it with them, but we refused.

Our guests smacked their lips and licked their fingers, rubbed their bellies and ate their fill. When night fell they let us go to our respective temporary homes and left with a bag full of chocolate bars and intentionally forged papers, which hopefully send them on as many false tracks as Papa had been able to invent.

It took many more hours before Papa succeeded in smuggling Uncle Frits, Aunt Kitty, and Ann out of their hiding place and on to their next address. Only then could he start thinking about means to help his friend Harry Romp, but hard as he tried he did not succeed. Harry Romp was executed on April 15th, 1945, a mere three weeks before the end of the war.

Hunger winter

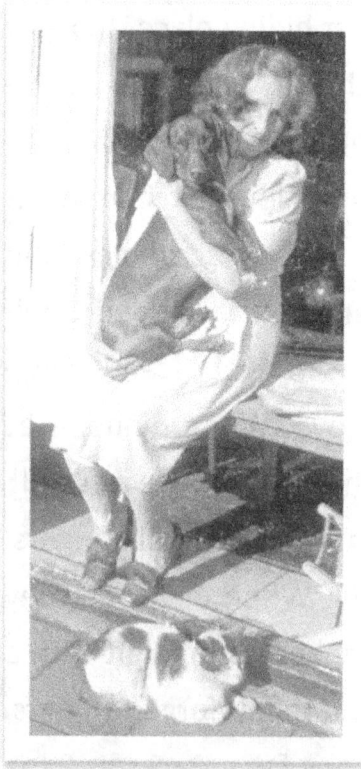
Mama with Fedia and Lioubka

The winter dragged on. People fed themselves on each other's dogs and cats and, if they were lucky, on rose hips and tulip bulbs.

Our own white and red cat Lioubka was one of the neighborhood's early victims. Our dog, Fedia, had been farmed out to Mama's mother when she herself went to the hospital, and escaped the slaughter.

Unfortunately, after the war my grandmother fed him so copiously that he died of overeating.

Aunt Ans Mertens still had a sack of maggoty flour with which she cooked water porridge every evening before allowing the fire to die. Those of us girls who hap-pened to be in the first school shift would tiptoe downstairs in the dark, eat the cold, sticky glue without salt or sugar, and trudge half an hour over the snow-covered dike in order to reach class before dawn.

On one such morning I walked over the abandoned dike. I was nearing the bridge where I had once seen a dead Jew, when a man on a bicycle came towards me. He rode slowly, probably because of the bad conditions of the road. The snow reflected enough moonlight for me to see that the man had a short, pointed beard. He was wearing glasses and a postman's cap. The nearer he came, the more he slowed down. I remembered Mama's warnings about wicked men who did unspecified, awful things to girls, and my blood froze. When the man was very close to me, he stopped his bicycle and stared at me without blinking. I wanted to run, but my feet were paralyzed. This is it, I knew. Now he is going to do 'it'.

It was then that the man took off his cap and glasses and said, "It's me, Papa. I wanted to check if my own daughter would recognize me in my disguise."

He had gone into hiding after the Germans had searched our home, but was still responsible for the upkeep of a great many Jews and could not stay inactive around the clock. On the morning I met him on the dike, he was on one of his eternal food hunts.

Papa at the beginning and the end of the war

Alexandra's Tenth Birthday

In the night before Alexandra's tenth birthday, I dreamt that Mama gave me her coral necklace, the one Papa had bought for her on the day I was born. "Thank you for this lovely daughter," he had said. And she, "Thank you for this lovely necklace. I will give it to Hannah when she gets married."

While I was dreaming, Mama died. At dawn Papa came and told us that she had passed away.

"Now I won't have to marry to get the coral necklace," I said to myself, and cried bitterly, not because I had lost my mother, but because of my evil thoughts. Aunt Ans, who otherwise was not expansive, took me in her bed and hugged me until I calmed down.

The last time we saw Mama, she lay in a cardboard box, dressed in what looked like a wedding gown. Although her Jewish identity was a secret even in death, Papa had insisted that her hands be folded loosely over her breast, rather than crossed as in Christian prayer. She looked like one of those expensive sleeping dolls I had always wished for my birthday.

Papa emerged from his hiding place for a few hours in order to bury his wife. He fastened a two-wheel vehicle to his bike without tires. On it he loaded the box, which he covered with a piece of black cloth. He steered the bike. Myriam and Alexandra walked to the left and right of our bride, and I trailed behind, holding on to the tail of the black cloth.

After the war Papa told us that Emmy Elffers-Andriesse had followed us with a gun in her handbag, and that he had made her promise she would shoot him right in the heart if the Germans arrested him. He had firmly decided to die on the spot rather than risk betraying Jews or fellow underground workers.

Long after my toes had become icicles, we were still trudging through the snow. I wondered if Papa knew how cold I was. I wondered if Mama was freezing in her bridal gown. I wondered if her soul was crawling through a tunnel or if it had grown wings and was flying in the air, which seemed appropriate, except for the fact that Papa had said 'passed away' and not 'flew away'. I wondered if the Germans would bother to kill a dead Jew if they caught one crawling to hell or flying to paradise. I wondered how long it would take to burn if you had to melt first. I thought of Mama, melting and burning. I wondered if she had reminded Papa about the coral necklace. I tried to cry but my tears froze.

We had left Amsterdam and were nearing the cemetery. As we plodded silently through the snow, a man on a bike caught up with us. "Hi, guys," he cheered, "what are you hiding in that big box? If you got hold of a piggy-pig by any chance, I'd like to share your dinner tonight."

We reached the cemetery and buried our doll, our Jew, our bride, our pig in a hole. A man filled the hole with earth and crossed himself. We waited until white snow had covered the black spot. After the funeral we plodded back through the snow to Amsterdam where we had some kind of lunch with Dick and Emmy Elffers. Before Papa went back into hiding, he gave me the coral necklace.

Two weeks later I turned twelve. Papa arrived with a loaf of white bread and half a pound of butter, distributed by the Swedish Red Cross. Although I shared the booty with everyone present, I swallowed down so much so fast that I threw it all up over the table. Aunt Ans didn't mind the mess, but cried because so much food was wasted.

In April Papa transferred his mutilated family to Amsterdam where we lived with Grethe who had lost her husband during the war. Papa was forty-two and Grethe thirty-nine. She had two daughters, Teeneke and Colette, who became our sisters.

On May 5th, 1945, the war was over. It ended as it had begun with foreign soldiers, fireworks and airplanes. Only this time the soldiers were called *yankees* instead of *krauts*, the fireworks were genuine, and the airplanes dropped food parcels. In May 1940 we had lived close enough to the National Airport 'Schiphol' to watch the opening moves of the war from our bedroom window.

In May 1945 we lived on the Stadionkade which was the last street of built-up Amsterdam, so that once again we had a front row view of the spectacle on the Sands. When I saw all that food, falling out of the sky right into the hands of the hungry masses, I finally understood what Parson Modderman meant when she told us about manna in the desert.

Living so close by the place where the action was, we were among the first to catch the tins of dry biscuits as they fell out of the sky.

Forty-five years later a tourist from Maryland, U.S.A., visited me and my family in Jerusalem. His name was Earl Griswold. When Mr Griswold heard that I was born in Amster-dam he said, "I was a fighter pilot during the Second World War. We used to fly over Ger-many and drop bombs, but when the war was over, we flew over Amsterdam and dropped tins of food. I never even knew what sort of food it was."

"You dropped them?" I cried out while falling in my guest's arms. "I picked them up! Biscuits! They were biscuits! Nothing ever tasted so good!"

Biscuits! Nothing ever tasted so good!

Back to Amstelveen

Papa returned to his job of Municipal Engineer of Amstelveen and was supposed to live within its borders, but strangers had moved into our house on the Rodenburghlaan. As great numbers of displaced persons were returning from Poland and Germany or emerging from their hiding places, homes were nearly impossible to get by. A huge concrete building on 511, Amsterdamse weg, stood empty. The Germans had used it for unmarried Dutch mothers of German babies.

In May 1945, the unmarried Dutch mothers were shaved bald and sent to Germany with their unwelcome offspring. The building was scrubbed clean of enemy dirt and allotted to the municipal engineer and his family. Grethe called the house 'Brouhaha' which is French for hubbub. Many years later, when I was already living in Jerusalem, I learned that the word *brouhaha* comes from the Hebrew *baruch haba*, welkom.

Although Papa and Grethe were not happy together, we girls had no reasons to complain. Each of us had a separate room, and all of us together had a flat roof as vast as a tennis court, and a living room in which Grethe organized concerts for dozens of her bohemian communist friends among whom Papa felt completely out of place. We also had a dense back garden in which we were allowed to keep pet animals, and which bordered on a canal so that in winter we could go ice skating straight from our home.

In addition to these luxuries, our 'Home for Unmarried Mothers' contained two little bathrooms, one with twelve tiny sinks, the other with five mini-potties on which Teeneke, Colette, Myriam, Alexandra and I sometimes sat in a row, peeing, shitting and crying with laughter.

Teeneke, Colette, Myriam, Alexandra and I in a row, peeing, shitting and crying with laughter.

Last but not least there was a basement in which we found thousands of booklets with pictures of Hitler as a newborn baby, Hitler as an adorable toddler, Hitler as an artistic teenager, Hitler as a romantic youngster, and Hitler as a military genius. Of all these Hitlers we made a gigantic bonfire in the garden. I regret that I didn't keep even one of these booklets as a memento, but at the time we wanted nothing more ardently than to destroy anything that reminded us of Hitler.

Aftermath of the War

After a while Papa and Grethe broke up their relationship. Papa quit his job at the municipality of Amstelveen, moved to Amersfoort and went into business, but he liked to play it big and was always short of money. Having spent his entire inheritance on rescuing Jews, he often relied on his sisters who helped him as much as they could. Never-the-less, the treasure he spotted at the horizon kept forever eluding him.

About the heroic deeds he had accomplished during the war he became as mute as a giraffe, that peaceful and friendly animal to which Mama used to compare him because of his height and exceptionally long neck. If he nevertheless agreed to tell us, his daughters, a thing or two, this happened by great exception and only in strict privacy.

Sometimes we were lucky enough to discover something by incident. Thus I was present, one day, when a stranger greeted Papa as Mr de Wit. Not only did Papa omit to correct him, but he even promised to transmit greetings to Mr van der Stad. Both names, Papa later told me, belonged to his long list of war names.

After the war some of Papa's protégé's wished him to be acknowledged by *Yad vaShem* as *Righteous among the Nations*, but Papa refused to receive honors for having done what he considered to be his duty.

He was extremely honored, however, when his Israeli son-in-law, the artist Abraham Yakin, created a four-meter-tall statue of a giraffe in the heart of Jerusalem.

During a well-attended naming ceremony, presided by the director of the Biblical Zoo, this statue received the name *Jan of Amersfoort*.

That this could be accomplished in 1959, when it was still absolutely forbidden to erect sculptures in Jerusalem, was due to a trick by the son-in-law, well worthy of the father-in-law, but that story belongs in another book.

Giraffe on the roof of the kiosk in Eliezer Playground, Ramban Street, Jerusalem.

תעודת כבוד
Certificate of Honour

THIS IS TO CERTIFY THAT IN ITS SESSION OF SEPTEMBER 29, 1997 THE COMMISSION FOR THE DESIGNATION OF THE RIGHTEOUS, ESTABLISHED BY YAD VASHEM, THE HOLOCAUST HEROES & MARTYRS' REMEMBRANCE AUTHORITY, ON THE BASIS OF EVIDENCE PRESENTED BEFORE IT, HAS DECIDED TO HONOUR

Jan Van Hulst — יאן ואן הולסט

WHO, DURING THE HOLOCAUST PERIOD IN EUROPE, RISKED HIS LIFE TO SAVE PERSECUTED JEWS.
THE COMMISSION, THEREFORE, HAS ACCORDED HIM THE MEDAL OF THE RIGHTEOUS AMONG THE NATIONS.
HIS NAME SHALL BE FOREVER ENGRAVED ON THE HONOUR WALL IN THE GARDEN OF THE RIGHTEOUS, AT YAD VASHEM, JERUSALEM.

Jerusalem, Israel
NOVEMBER 16, 1997

ON BEHALF OF THE YAD VASHEM DIRECTORATE

ON BEHALF OF THE COMMISSION FOR THE DESIGNATION OF THE RIGHTEOUS

Afterword

Twenty-two years after Papa's death, Rudie Reisel insisted again that Papa be honored by Yad Vashem.

Alexandra said "No" because Papa had not wanted it during his life. I said "Yes" because in Judaism the living have priority above the dead and Rudy found it hard to conclude his own life without having officially expressed his gratitude to his rescuer.

It was Myriam who, after due consideration, proposed that we should agree to have Papa's name mentioned in the *Lexicon of the Righteous among the Nations*, but decline to receive a medal in his name.

Thus, on September 29th, 1997, *the Commission for the Designation of the Righteous among the Nations, established by Yad Vashem, the Holocaust Heroes' and Martyrs' Remembrance Authority in Jerusalem*, officially honored Jan van Hulst, who during the Holocaust had risked his life to save persecuted Jews, with the title *Righteous among the Nations*.

Papa holding baby Hannah

Myriam, Mama holding baby Hannah

Left to right: Alexandra, Myriam and Hannah with the necklaces Jan gave Paula at the birth of their daughters.

Alexandra and Myriam visiting Israel in honor of Hannah's 80th birthday.

Patricia O'Donovan's puppet show "Jan's Daughter" is based on the story in this book. Patricia performs in English, French, Hebrew and Spanish. For information please go to patod3@googlemail.com

Patricia on stage during the play "Jan's Daughter".

The puppets on the right are Hannah's 'family'.

Myriam and Alexandra with Patricia's puppets (the family) during a Puppet Festival in Meppel, the Netherlands.

For other books by Hannah Yakin see:

www.art-yakin.com – HANNAH - books

www.ingramcontent.com/pod-product-compliance
Lightning Source LLC
LaVergne TN
LVHW021613080426
835510LV00019B/2552